Contents

Growing plants

This book is all about growing different kinds of plants. You will find out that plants can be grown in several ways, and you will also find out what seeds need to make them grow.

Different plants survive from one year to the next in different ways. Some die after a few months, but they make seeds which will grow into new plants. Others, such as trees, can stay alive for many years. Some plants, such as rhubarb, die back every autumn and the leaves die. The plant grows again in the spring.

Above *This dandelion flower has died and made seeds.*

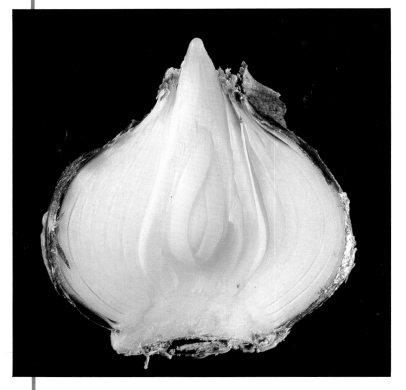

Hyacinths make underground food stores called bulbs. Bulbs grow into new plants the next year. We can't eat hyacinth bulbs. They are poisonous. But we can eat the food in an onion bulb.

Left *The inside of a hyacinth bulb. It looks like an onion bulb but it is poisonous.*

In this book there are lots of different activities to try. You don't need a garden for any of the growing projects, but a window-box would be useful.

Remember to be patient. Plants sometimes take a very long time to grow. But it will be worth it when you show friends your own plants which you have grown from seeds or cuttings.

All sorts of plants and flowers can be grown in a window-box.

Read these notes carefully before you start:

1 Always remember that plants are alive. They need to be looked after if they are to grow well.

2 Read through each activity before you start, to make sure you have everything you need.

3 Ask permission before you take cuttings, pick flowers, or use tools or utensils.

4 Wash your hands before and after handling plants and compost.

5 Water your plants when the compost starts to feel dry, but don't drown them! Put your finger in the soil down to just past your fingernail. If the soil feels dry, the plant needs water.

If there is water in the tray thirty seconds after you have watered the plant, empty the tray.

6 Use pots with holes in the bottom and put pebbles over the holes. Place trays under the pots.

7 Wash all the tools and pots you have used for plants with hot, soapy water.

You could keep all the things you use for growing plants together in a cardboard box.

8 Always wash plants that can be eaten before you use them in cooking.

What's in a plant?

Most plants are made in the same way, whatever their size. Look carefully at this picture of a geranium.

Plants need sunlight to make their food. Inside each leaf there are lots of cells, which are like mini 'factories'.

The cells use sunlight to join water and carbon dioxide together. This makes food for the plant.

This is what cells would look like close up.

The stem holds the plant up. It carries water and nutrients from the roots to the leaves.

Plants take carbon dioxide from the air.

The flowers make seeds, which can grow into new plants.

The leaves grow from the stem.

The plant grows roots down into the ground. The roots work their way through the soil and hold the plant in place.

Roots take in water and nutrients from the soil. Nutrients keep the plant healthy, a bit like the way vitamins keep people healthy.

Germinating seeds

When a seed germinates, it begins to grow into a new plant. You can see little roots at the bottom and some leaves at the top.

Try this investigation to find out if cress seeds need light to germinate.

You will need:
- 3 saucers
- cotton wool
- packet of cress seeds
- egg cup or measuring jug
- water
- slightly see-through plastic box, such as an ice-cream carton
- cardboard box with no holes
- ruler

1 Spread a thin layer of cotton wool on the bottom of each saucer.

2 Carefully put ten cress seeds on to the cotton wool in each saucer.

3 Pour a little water on to each saucer using an egg cup or a measuring jug.

4 Put the saucers on a sunny windowsill. Leave one uncovered so that lots of light reaches these seeds. Put an empty ice-cream box over the next saucer. Some light will get to these seeds. Put a cardboard box over the last saucer. No light will reach these seeds.

5 Check your seeds every day. If the cotton wool feels dry, then pour on a little more water.

6 After a week, count how many seeds have germinated in each saucer. Measure how tall the plants have grown with a ruler.

In which saucer did the most seeds germinate? Which seeds grew the tallest during the whole time? Which plants looked the most healthy? Are the tall plants the healthiest? So, do cress seeds need light to germinate?

Draw a chart like this to record your measurements:

Where the seeds were	How many germinated	Height of plants
sunny windowsill		
under ice-cream box		
under cardboard box		

Here are some more ideas to investigate:
1 Does temperature make a difference to how well the plants grow?
2 Does the amount of water make a difference?
3 Is soil better than cotton wool? Make a fair test to investigate one of these ideas.

Small seeds and big trees

Seeds come in all sorts of shapes and sizes. All seeds can grow into new plants if you look after them properly. This is how to grow small seeds.

You will need:
- seed tray, or an old ice-cream box with holes in the bottom – ask an adult to made the holes
- seed compost
- trowel
- water
- packet of flower seeds
- newspaper
- clingfilm

Different kinds of seeds: clockwise from top left: mung beans, kidney beans, coconut (inset), avocado, poppy seeds.

1 Fill the tray nearly to the top with seed compost.

2 Put the tray on some layers of newspaper – do this outdoors if possible. Pour water all over the compost until it is wet through. Let the extra water run out.

3 Sprinkle the seeds all over the surface of the compost.

4 Cover the seeds with a thin layer of dry compost. Seeds germinate best in a warm place. (Some seeds need to be kept in the dark – check the seed packet.) Ask if you can use an airing cupboard or a place near a boiler.

6 When the seedlings are just touching the clingfilm, take it off. Put the tray in a sunny place to let the seedlings grow.

When the seedlings are bigger they need to be moved into pots or put outside in a window-box or garden. (See page 13 for how to put small plants into pots.)

5 Cover the tray with clingfilm. You don't need to water the seeds until they have germinated.

This oak tree grew from an acorn. It probably took one hundred years to grow this big.

It takes a very long time to grow a tree from a seed. Put an acorn or an apple pip in a pot with some compost. Keep the compost moist. If you are lucky and your seed germinates, find a safe place outside and plant your seedling there in the autumn. One day your tree will be taller than you are!

New plants from old

The mother of millions makes baby plants around its leaves. These drop off and can grow separately. If you take a small piece from a plant, it sometimes grows into a new plant. This is called taking a cutting. Spider plants, geraniums and tradescantia are all easy plants to take cuttings from.

You will need:
- large, healthy plant
- sharp scissors
- tall glass jar
- potting compost
- clean plant pots

(or yogurt cartons with holes made in the bottom – ask an adult to do this)
- pencil
- trowel

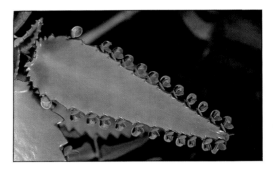

The leaf of a mother of millions plant with baby plants on it.

1 Ask the person who owns the plant if you may take a cutting.

2 Find a section of the plant about 10 cm long. Carefully cut it off the plant at the joint, using scissors.

3 Take the leaves off the bottom 3 cm of the cutting. Snip one centimetre off the very top. Take off any flowers or side branches as well.

4 Put your cutting into the glass jar. Pour some water into the jar so that it just reaches the plant. Leave it in a sunny place until little white roots start to grow. Make sure the water always reaches the plant.

5 Fill the pot with potting compost.

6 Make a hole in the compost with a pencil.

8 Water the plant carefully.

7 Gently place the cutting in the hole and push the compost around the stem so the cutting is held upright. Make sure the roots are covered.

You might want to make more than one cutting. Remember to water your cuttings regularly. After a few weeks some may have died, but one or two may have started to grow new leaves. You will have grown a whole new plant from just a tiny cutting. It will be just the same as the plant that it came from.

Growing beans

You can grow any dried beans from your kitchen cupboard – try red kidney beans or broad beans. Beans are the seeds of bean plants. Runner beans have the biggest seeds. Here is an interesting way to grow them.

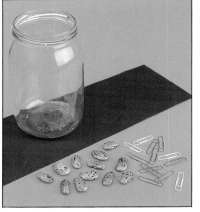

You will need:
- wide-necked jar or drinking glass
- long strip of black paper, about 60 cm long and about the same
- width as the height of your jar
- water
- twelve bean seeds
- paperclips

1 Soak the paper in water for a few seconds. Then let it drain for a while.

2 Put one bean at the end of the paper and roll it up a short way.

3 Put another bean on the paper and roll this one up too.

14

4 Keep on adding beans and rolling until all the beans are rolled into the paper.

5 Make sure the roll is as tight as possible – don't let the beans drop out!

6 Now fit the roll into the jar. If it is too loose use two paperclips to hold the roll tight.

7 Put the jar on a sunny windowsill. Check your beans every day and make sure the water is always 1 cm deep.

8 After a few weeks the beans will have grown into plants. Then they can be put into big pots. These children are following the instructions on page 13 for potting plants.

Potted potatoes

You can grow potatoes in a pot indoors. It takes about four months from start to finish. You need an old potato that is starting to grow little shoots. You could buy special seed potatoes for this.

You will need:
- big pot or old bucket, about 30 cm wide at the top and at least 30 cm deep
- potting compost from a grow-bag
- trowel
- potato with shoots
- old tray or lots of old newspapers
- plastic sack

1 Fill up the pot with compost. Dig a hole 15 cm deep in the compost.

2 Put the potato in the bucket. The side with the most shoots should be pointing upwards.

3 Cover the potato with compost.

4 Put the pot on an old tray or on lots of layers of newspaper. Water the pot until the compost is moist. Put the pot somewhere sunny but not in everybody's way!

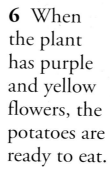

6 When the plant has purple and yellow flowers, the potatoes are ready to eat.

7 Do this part outdoors if possible because it is very messy! If you have to do it inside, first spread out lots of newspaper or a plastic sack. Pull the whole plant out of the pot and lay it on the ground. Dig around and pull out all the potatoes. Then tidy up.

5 Water the potato each time the compost feels dry. After a while you will see a dark green plant beginning to grow. If you see any potatoes, cover them over with more compost.

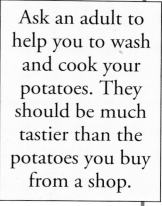

Ask an adult to help you to wash and cook your potatoes. They should be much tastier than the potatoes you buy from a shop.

Floral displays

Most flowers are very pretty. A bouquet of flowers is made by putting lots of different flowers together. It's nice to be given flowers because they smell good and they brighten up a room. A bunch of flowers only lasts a few days. The flowers have been cut so they have no roots, and they will soon die.

You might have seen a floral display in a park or garden. To make a floral display, many plants are grown from seeds or bulbs. When they are seedlings they are planted in the soil. Plants with different-coloured flowers are planted next to each other to make patterns. These plants will make new flowers for many months. The floral display looks good all summer.

Above *This girl is giving her grandmother a beautiful bunch of flowers.*

Right *A floral display in Canberra, Australia.*

You can grow your own floral display. Choose two kinds of seeds which will make different-coloured flowers. Use seeds for small plants, such as alyssum (yellow or white) and lobelia (red, blue, yellow or white). Or try growing marigolds, pansies or petunias.

Look at pages 10–11 for how to grow seeds. When you reach number 3 in the instructions, sprinkle one kind of seed to make a pattern. Then fill the rest of the tray with the other seeds. You could try the patterns below, or make up your own pattern.

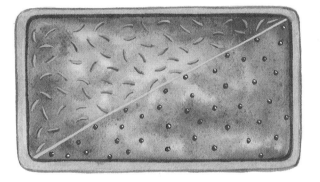

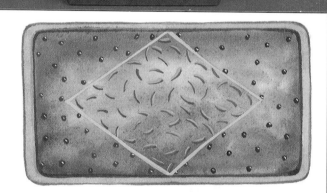

When your seeds have grown into plants, you will have your own floral display.

Plant medicines

Some plants have special chemicals in them which can be used to make medicines. Over time, people have found out which plants are safe and how much of the plant to use. Some plants are very poisonous and must not be eaten.

Plant medicines are called herbal remedies. Perhaps you sometimes drink herbal tea. Camomile tea is made from camomile flowers soaked in boiling water. The tea is said to relax you.

Above
These girls are picking camomile flowers.

Left
A rosemary bush.

Rosemary is a common garden bush. Rosemary plants produce an oil that smells fresh and herby. If you have a rosemary bush, squeeze a few leaves between your fingers to get a really strong smell. Aromatherapists use rosemary oil to help people who have headaches.

Tangerine oil helps people to feel more cheerful. Do you know of other plants that have a strong smell?

Some plants are used to make strong medicine to help people who are very ill. You should never try these. A drug called morphine can be made from poppies. Morphine is a pain-killer. A drug to help people who have something wrong with their hearts is made from foxgloves.

Above A field of poppies.

Left A willow tree.

Below Close-up of the bark of a willow tree. A substance in the bark is used to make aspirin tablets.

Aspirin, which people take to bring down a high temperature, can be made from the bark of the willow tree.

Making a lavender bag

Before air fresheners were invented, people used lavender baskets and other scented herbs to make clothes and rooms smell nicer. Put a lavender bag in a drawer and soon your clothes will have a lavender scent.

You will need:

- bunch of dried lavender flowers
- piece of thin, patterned material about 30 cm long and 15 cm wide
- sewing needle and some pins
- cotton
- elastic band
- piece of ribbon about 30 cm long

1 Pull off flowers from the lavender stalks until you have about a cupful.

2 Fold the material in half with the wrong side out. Fold over the top 3 cm on one side to make a flap. Turn the pouch over and fold down the top 3 cm to make a flap on the other side.

3 Pin down the sides of the pouch, making sure the flaps stay folded down.

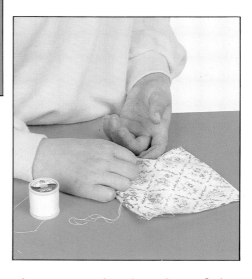

4 Sew up both sides of the pouch.

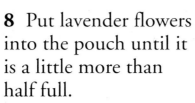

8 Put lavender flowers into the pouch until it is a little more than half full.

5 Pin the first flap to the material beneath it. Don't pin through to the other side of the pouch! Then turn the pouch over and pin down the other flap in the same way.

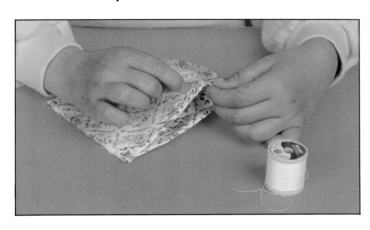

9 Tie the pouch tightly with an elastic band.

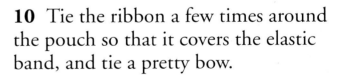

6 Sew one of the flaps to the material beneath it. Then do the same on the other side.

10 Tie the ribbon a few times around the pouch so that it covers the elastic band, and tie a pretty bow.

7 Turn the pouch inside out so that the right side of the material is outwards.

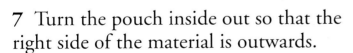

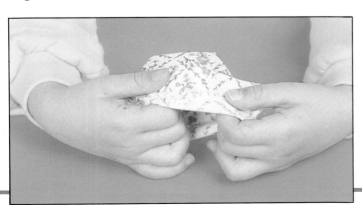

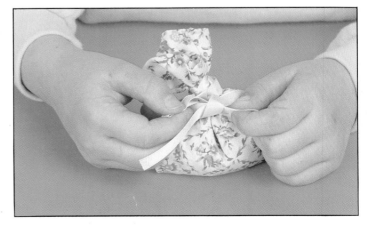

Forcing bulbs

Many people love flowers and plants. You can give plants to friends who don't have gardens. In the winter you could give a bowl of hyacinths or daffodils. These flowers do not usually come out until the spring, but you can trick them into coming out early.

If you put the bulbs in a cold place and then in a warm place they will 'think' that it was winter and now it is spring. This is called forcing bulbs. Start about three months before you need the bulbs to flower.

To force bulbs you will need:
- pretty bowl or pot
- pebbles
- 3–5 bulbs
- compost
- large plastic bag
- fridge

2 Put a layer of compost into the bowl.

1 Make sure the bowl has holes in the bottom. Put some pebbles over the holes.

3 Water the compost.

4 Arrange the bulbs so that the tops point upwards. Cover them over with more compost. The bulbs should be buried at least 5 cm deep.

5 Carefully place the whole bowl inside the plastic bag. Tie the bag and put it in the fridge. Leave the bulbs in the fridge for eight weeks. You don't need to do anything to them at all. (Your bulbs will 'think' it is winter.)

6 Take the bowl out and take off the plastic bag. Put it somewhere cool. Maybe you have a cold lobby or porch? Stand the bowl on a saucer and water it every few days. (Your bulbs now 'think' it is the beginning of spring.)

7 After a week bring the bulbs into a warm room. They should soon begin to grow. They will be ready to flower after another two or three weeks.

Here you can see how hyacinth bulbs grow shoots and then flowers.

Pressing flowers

You can keep flowers by pressing them. Small flowers and leaves with few veins press well. Pick a few of several different kinds of flowers – but ask the person they belong to first!

You will need:

- different kinds of flowers
- some blotting paper
- newspaper
- some very heavy books
- card to stick the flowers on
- glue
- sticky-back plastic

1 Lay the flowers carefully on the blotting paper.

2 Put another piece of blotting paper on top.

3 Open a big, heavy book and put some newspaper on the open page. Slide the sheets of blotting paper with the flowers inside them on to the newspaper. Put some more newspaper on top.

4 Close the book gently then press it firmly closed. Leave the book under some other heavy books for about a month.

If your flowers have been carefully pressed they will be as thin as tissue paper.

5 You can now glue each flower on to a piece of stiff card. Be careful not to damage the flowers.

6 When the glue has dried, cover each card in sticky-back plastic. You could give the cards as bookmarks.

You might like to paint a garden and stick real pressed flowers on to the painting.

Making a herb garden

Herbs are plants that have a strong smell or a strong taste. They are used to add flavour to food. You can grow herbs in a garden but many people grow them indoors in pots. If the pots are kept in the kitchen, it is easy to pick fresh herbs to use in cooking.

Mint is a very easy herb to grow. You can use mint to make a glass of lemonade look and taste special.

Ask someone who has a mint bush for a cutting so that you can grow your own plant. Follow the instructions on pages 12–13 for taking cuttings.

You can also take cuttings of rosemary. This herb is often used with roast lamb.

Rosemary is harder to grow. Take lots of cuttings and hopefully a few will grow.

Here are some common herbs that you could try to grow.

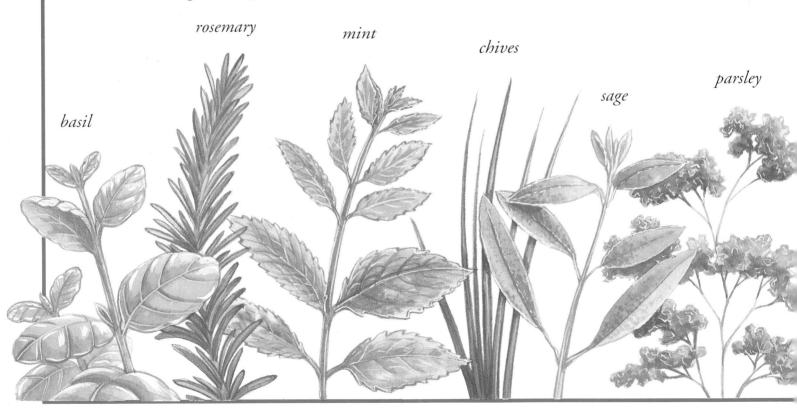

basil rosemary mint chives sage parsley

Chives can be chopped up small and put into potato salad. Basil goes well with fresh tomatoes and onions in a salad. Sage tastes good in winter soups.

Follow the instructions on pages 10–11 to grow chives, sage or basil from seeds. When the herb plants are a few centimetres tall they are ready to be put into pots. You can use small yoghurt pots with holes in the bottom.

You can see basil seedlings at the front and sage seedlings at the back of the seed tray.

A child is carefully taking a sage seedling out of the seed tray to plant it in a pot.

Be very careful when you take the plants out of the seed tray or you will pull their roots off and they will die. Use a spoon to dig the whole plant up from underneath. Hold the plant by its leaves only. Never touch the roots.

Fill each yogurt pot with potting compost. Make a hole in the compost with a pencil. Then place the little plant in the hole. Push the compost around the stem so that the cutting is held upright. (See page 13 for pictures showing how to do this.)

If you have enough plants left over you could make a windowsill herb garden for someone else.

Glossary

Aromatherapists People who practise aromatherapy, a special branch of medicine that uses the scent of plants.

Bouquet A bunch of flowers.

Bulbs The food store of a new plant, with the shoot inside. It is a rounded shape and it is underground.

Compost Soil that is specially prepared to help plants to grow. It has all the nutrients in it that plants need.

Cutting A small part of a plant that can grow into a new plant.

Floral display A display of brightly-coloured flowers growing in a big flowerbed.

Germination When a seed sprouts and begins to grow into a new plant.

Herbal remedies Medicines that are made from plants.

Herbs Plants that usually have a strong smell and are used in cookery and in medicine.

Nutrients Chemicals found in the soil that a plant needs for it to grow.

Roots The underground parts of a plant that hold it in place and take in water and nutrients from the soil.

Seedling A very young plant with just a few leaves.

Stem The upright part of a plant that holds up the leaves and flowers.

Veins The pipes inside a leaf that carry water and nutrients from the stem to all the parts of the leaf.

Finding out more

Crafty Ideas with Growing Things by Melanie Rice (Hodder and Stoughton, 1991)

Green Fingers Activity Book by Peter Eldin (Hippo Books, 1991)

Kid's Book of Gardening: Growing Plants Indoors and Out by Derek Fell (Running Press, USA, 1991)

Gardening: In and Out by Jan Morrow (Longman, 1990)

Growing it for Fun by Denny Robson (Franklin Watts, 1991)

Get Growing: Exciting Indoor Plant Projects for Kids by Lois Walker (Wiley, 1991)

Growing Things by Angela Wilkes (Usborne Publishers, 1989)

My First Garden Book by Angela Wilkes (Dorling Kindersley, 1992)

Acknowledgements
The publishers would like to thank the following for permission to reproduce photographs in this book: Ardea London (J M Labat) 4 (below), 5; Biofotos (Heather Angel) 18 (right), 21 (top and bottom left), 29 (both); Bruce Coleman (H Lange) 11 (below right), (E Pott) 17 (top right); Natural History Picture Agency (G Bernard) 21 (below right) and 25 (bottom left and centre), (G Gainsburgh) 25 (bottom right); Natural Science Photos (G Beckett) 20 (left); OSF (B P Kent) 12 (top right), (S Morris) 20 (right); Still Pictures (T Barrett) 4 (above); Wayland (Z Mukhida) *cover*, 14-15.
The photographs on pages 8-9, 10, 11 (except bottom right), 12 (except top right), 13, 16-17, 19 (above right), 22-3, 24, 25 (top left and right), 26-7 were taken by APM Photographic.

The artwork on the cover and on pages 6-7, 19 and 28 (below) is by Jackie Harland. We would like to thank the staff and children at Somerhill Junior School, Hove, Sussex, for their kind assistance.

Index

A 'g' shows that the word is in the glossary.